Appleseeds

Or, How We Got Here
An Anthology of Americana Poetry

Editing and Lay-Out by
Melissa Guillet

Cover Design by
Eric Urban

Sacred Fools Press

APPLESEEDS
Or, How We Got Here
An Anthology of Americana Poetry

Foreword © 2008 Melissa Guillet
Copyright © 2008 Sacred Fools Press

All poems' copyrights are held by their authors. No part may be reprinted without the author's written permission.

All rights reserved. No part of this book may be reproduced or transmitted in any form without written permission from the publisher, except by reviewers who may quote brief exerpts in connection with a review.

Printed in the United States of America.

ISBN: 978-0-615-24970-4 pbk.

Published by Sacred Fools Press
45 Dean Avenue
Johnston, RI 02919

Layout by Melissa Guillet
Cover Art and Design by Eric Urban

Text Set in Eurostile, Optima, and Times Roman.

Table of Contents

Foreword   *ix*

	Author	Americana Poem	Page
1.	Sharon Lynn Griffiths	Johnny Appleseed	1
2.	John Flynn	In Praise of Boston Aunts	3
3.	Tom Chandler	Jerimoth Hill	4
4.	Jean Meyer Aloe	Nightmare on Route 1	5
5.	Paul Hamill	Carolina Honey	6
6.	Melissa Guillet	The Memory Garden	8
7.	Jim Lanier	It's More Like Herding Ghosts Than Cats	9
8.	Pete Dolack	Redwoods	10
9.	F.I. Goldhaber	The Mall	11
10.	Pete Dolack	Black Hills	12
11.	Lucille Lang Day	710 Ashbury, 1967	15
12.	Marty McConnell	Geometry of the Obvious	16
13	Joanne Lowery	Saving Abe	17
14.	Valerie Lawson	Don't Tread On Me	18
15.	Anne Brudevold	Seascape	20
16.	Jennifer Wallace	A Slow-filling Cloud	22
17.	Gretchen Fletcher	Too Blue Skies	24
18.	David Wolf	Maneuvers	26
19.	Bruce Weber	Toy Soldiers	27
20.	Artie Moffa	Stereo Sun	28
21.	Stephen Lindow	Dryer	34
22.	Lewis Gardner	A Gift from Great-Aunt Prudence	35
23.	Bob Hoeppner	Picnic	36
24.	Gretchen Fletcher	Ah, Yes, the Fourth	37
25.	Madeline Artenberg	Chosen Seats	38
26.	Ted Giovannini	For Nonna	40
27.	Tony Brown	Where Do You Live?	41
28.	Michele Sackman	The Quilting Bee	44
29.	Kim Roberts	"Lyda E. Pinkham's Vegetable Compound"	46
30.	Wendy Vardaman	Roosters and Hens	47
31.	Thomas D. Jones	A Bagger's Life	49
32.	Laura Lee Washburn	S & H Green Stamps	51
33.	Lewis Gardner	Pennies	53

34. Ryk McIntyre	Penny Candy Store	54
35. Jeff Poniewaz	Turkey in the Straw for Charles Ives	55
36. Hal Sirowitz	Where the Buffalo Went	56
37. Kim Roberts	New Haven	57
38. Helen Ruggieri	The Last Performing Wallendas	58
39. Elizabeth Kerlikowske	Jane's Shadow Family	59
40. Lenore Weiss	Ode to Emeril	61
41. Suzanne Frank	On Losing Faith	63
42. David Lawton	Johnny Cash	64
43. Julia Gordon-Bramer	Viva Las Vegas	65
44. David Lee Summers	Racing Amtrak	67
45. Sarah Getty	Rocks, Utah	68
46. Victoria Muñoz	Fresco From Summer	70
47. Bill MacMillan	Fayetteville to Memphis	71
48. Linda O'Connell	Wanderlust	73
49. Jade Sylvan	Back Home	75
50. Anne Brudevold	The Ride	78
51. Lori Desrosiers	Jalopy	80
52. Lori Desrosiers	The Gear-Head's Wife's Lament	80
53. Tom Bird	Shop Talk	81
54. Amy MacLennan	The Beauty Shop	82
55. Lyn Lifshin	Barbie Looks Up Her Birthday	84
56. Sheila Mullen Twyman	On the Fourth Day	86
57. Timothy Mason	Baseball Cards	88
58. Charles Salmons	On the 100th Anniversary of the World Series	90
59. Caridad McCormick	Things I Didn't Know I Loved	91
60. Kit Wallach	Johnny Appleseed	93

Contributor Notes	97
Acknowledgments	107

Foreword

by Melissa Guillet

In putting together this anthology, I never anticipated how broadly interpreted "Americana" would be. After sifting through a plethora of road trip poems, I chose poems that showed America as it was: the land, the people, the cultures and traditions brought over by immigrants, the icons and pastimes that would influence generations, the metaphorical and literal power of the automobile, the colors and symbols of America. I also included some of its now: celebrity and hunger for fame, commercialism, natural and man-made wonders. This anthology by no means includes every voice America has. Some groups I hoped to repesent did not share poems. Others sent poems that could have been a book in themselves or strayed too far from where most of the poems were coming from. An anthology just on America's historical figures may be forthcoming... But it was America's people, the experiences they could have only had here, that I most wanted to represent. Nostalgic stories of the past. Hopes for the future. The seeds of the "American Dream."

Appleseeds

Sharon Lynn Griffiths

Johnny Appleseed

They say he came to Pennsylvania
not the hard and dirty Pittsburgh we know,
but a younger place—impressionable enough
to remember him and pass his story on.

Born in Boston, they say he was,
and the first thing his blue eyes focused on:
a lacy rill of apple blossoms outside his nursery window,
just before the Battle of Bunker Hill
would send them flying through sulfur smoke,
living confetti that fell and withered in red mud.

He built a house on Pittsburgh's Hump
and down along the gentle slopes he planted
apple trees that erupted in great showers
of pink and white snow every spring.
They say that bees came from all around
for the privilege of turning the pollen into honey.
And he didn't charge his neighbors for it
because, he said, the bees didn't charge him to make it.

His great kind heart and head were cracked, they say,
by some flighty child who set her sights on things
more practical than apples. So he picked up and left her,
dragging two canoes full of apple seeds to the river.

Ohio turned to Muskingum, then he followed it
to White Woman Creek, stopping often
to pour fragrant black seeds
into farmer's puzzled hands.
And when he ran out, along Licking Creek,
he turned and went back for more.

One hundred thousand square miles
of pink and white snow
grew and sparkled in clear spring skies,
gave sweet shade and breezes in summer,
gave sweet fruit and honey in autumn and winter.

One hundred thousand square miles in Ohio and Indiana—
Shadeland, Coolspring, Mansfield, and on
to the banks of the Wabash.
Finally to Fort Wayne, never to wake
after a twenty-mile walk, a visit
with a friend, and a story from the Bible—
the one he called "the news fresh from Heaven"
and we call the Sermon on the Mount.

They say he got stranger as time went on—
took to wearing nothing but a coffee sack,
barefoot even in snow, a tin kettle on his head.
They say the Indians were kind to him—
that he could play with bear cubs
while their mother looked on,
that he was welcome at the tables
of grateful farmers but would not eat
'til he was sure there was enough for the children.

When he died, Sam Houston made a speech in Congress,
called him "one of the most useful citizens of the world."
And he bid farewell to a "dear old eccentric heart,"
saying that "generations yet unborn will call you blessed."

And I know they did—those generations—
as they took in the beauty and the bounty
of one hundred thousand square miles of apple trees.
At least until those trees were broken,
pushed over and plowed under for strip malls,
and highways, and other such mundane sadness.

John Flynn

In Praise of Boston Aunts

Most of that part of town is gentrified or simply gone.

Walking the surly brick neighborhoods of the North End
I imagine it's 1964. President Kennedy
the man I was named after is officially dead.
In *The European* restaurant,
Perry Como and Vaughn Monroe
croon out of the jukebox.
Aunts Louise, Etta, and Anna play hopscotch.
I trace them back to Holy Days,
Monsignors and hopeful pews,
Masses in Latin when weddings were easier
to trust.
Crème de menthe over spumoni a rare treat
that made losses endurable for a time.

I walk to Haymarket Square.
My aunts in crinoline dresses
fill paper bags with cherries,
smile at me and point to Boston
Harbor where the SS Cretic
unloads their illiterate Papa
Mama, destiny.

For a moment, I can smell immigrant laughter,
tears of *aventura* and arrival.

Tom Chandler

Jerimoth Hill
812 feet, the highest point in Rhode Island

You will not recognize any bald knob of granite
or sheer cliff face silhouetted against clouds,
in fact, you won't realize you're anywhere at all
except by this bullet-riddled sign by the road
that curves through these scraggled third growth
woods that was once a grove of giant pines
that were cut down for masts that were used
to build ships to sail away to the rest of the world
from the docks of Providence Harbor, their holds
filled with wool from the sheep that grazed
in the field that had once been the giant pines
till the shepherds died off and the applers took over
and grew orchards of Cortlands and Macintosh
Delicious to fill the holds of the ships that sailed
to the rest of the world from the docks of Providence
Harbor with masts made from the giant pines till
the orchards moved west along with everything
else to less glacial land and the fields became
overgrowth of berries and hobblebush crisscrossed
by walls made of stones that had slept beneath
one inch of topsoil for twelve thousand years
till the settlers found when they tried to plant crops
that this was a country that grew only rocks which
they made into walls to pen in the sheep that provided
the wool that filled the holds of the ships that sailed
to the rest of the world from the docks of Providence Harbor.

Jean Meyer Aloe

Nightmare on Route 1

Undulating like an earthworm,
The dream humps me past my life
Displayed on decaying billboards
In succinct one-liners.
Like those Burma Shave clichés
We passed every winter,
Driving seventy-two hours
Non-stop down Route 1
From Jersey City to Ft. Lauderdale:
Smile even though it hurts.
Don't bleed on the carpet.
Happiness is only a day away.
They slip by in slow motion,
Fade into black like a bad movie.
At the Stuckey's rest stops,
We bought pecan pralines
That stuck to our teeth. Mother
made us brush after every meal.

Paul Hamill

Carolina Honey

Thunder and lightning near my house
And in the morning a split tree, dazed bees
And a massive seam of honey. I grabbed a bucket
And took a big slab of comb, exhilarated:
An open treasure chest, a bear's adventure,
A theft like pears from the mean neighbor's tree
—Who knows what parts of boyhood glee and greed
Buzzed in my heart as I grabbed before the bees
Could muster? I warmed the comb on the kitchen stove.
The flow was dark and languid, rich on my spoon tip,
Glazed at the surface.   I sat by the stove thinking
Of a friend who had been switching—not caught, more like
A sipping bee—between two women, one
Swept by dark moods but passionate, who came
And left and came and left the city, as if
Gathering nectar for a far hive; the other
Sweet and simpler, to whom he always homed,
Whose patience puzzled me.   I thought of swarms,
Soft petals, inexplicable commutes,
And how bees carry more than they know.

Then I looked up. My back door screen and windows
Were dark with a carpet of bees, eerily silent
But stuck to the cloying scent at the mesh   It felt
Like a thousand voyeurs, a wall of paparazzi
Creeping over each other. I saw I must
Be wary, make furtive exits, wait for dark,
Be alert for the jealous whine of an intruder.

Just then my friend came in through the bee-less front
Of the house, and said in the suggesting way
Men have with peers, especially in the South,

"Don't think I'd feed the kids that." "No?" "That tree
Was in the big azalea garden. Those flowers
Have something paralytic in them, small kids
Die eating them." "You sure?" "About the honey?
No. Read it somewhere. Might be wrong. Still."
I capped the pot, and in the cool of night
When most of the thick mat of bees had left
And a quick flip of the door knocked off the rest
I dumped the gluey mass near where I got it:
No use to bees now, but maybe a raccoon
Would leave my trash and get a belly-ache.
Next day, my neighbor smiled a complicit grin:
"Man's gotta be careful where he gits his honey."

Melissa Guillet

The Memory Garden

Grass replaces asphalt..
Weeds whittle through the cracks
of winter coughs and heaves.
Broken glass glints green and grows:
The compost of drinking teens.

Crashed space saucers –
burnt out parking lights –
dangle over the metallic stray hairs
of headless speaker stands.

Tattered screen shows more sky than showcase:
a behemoth postcard
without picture or address.
The movies have all gone
to video or ash can.
No more backing up the station wagon.
No more overpriced sodas.
No more restroom intermission lines
or sweaty popcorn palms.

Over a garden of gravel and crushed cans,
the blossoming ends of soaked cigarette butts,
soda tabs, twist-off caps, a soulless kite,
grow the clover, the dandelions,
the milkweed and trees planted by birds.

The merry-go-round still spins,
groaning with the ghosts of laughter.
Landscaped by the wind, the past drifts
and returns, drifts and returns,
memories stuck like old chewing gum.

Jim Lanier

It's More Like Herding Ghosts Than Cats

As I blow out the park lot
I don't so much see trash
As ghosts of pleasures past.
Cigarette butts, cellophane,
Candy wrappers, panties.
Ah, the pleasure!
Ah, the death.

Pete Dolack

Redwoods

Two women in an SUV roll up next to me
And ask where are the redwood trees
Where can we drive past the trees?
You have to hike to see them
I reply
Without adding that
There aren't many redwoods left
Yesterday I had to hike eight miles both ways
To see the grove of the tallest redwoods
The logging companies graciously left behind
When the forecast of 12 mills
Cutting for 1,000 years
Proved a trifle optimistic
Maybe the visitors' center can give you directions
I suggest
And the SUV road warriors drive off
I see a few more redwoods this afternoon
Although everything grows so big here
The world's tallest
But still not big enough
To sate a gargantuan appetite

F.I. Goldhaber

The Mall

The shopping mall barricades
itself from me and the walk
with densely planted shrubs
and endless rows of parked cars.

Pedestrians are not welcome
here and take their lives in hand
attempting to navigate
in through vehicle access points.

They've painted paths
bright yellow leading into
the cavernous altars of
the god of consumerism.

When I leave, drivers
follow me halfway down the aisle;
speed past as I keep walking,
looking for a closer parking spot.

Pete Dolack

Black Hills

An island on the Plains is
America in microcosm
Natural beauty and insult
Packaged for instant consumption
Both are first seen at a distance
The endless signs dappled
Onto sunflower fields and ranches along Highway 90
Ceaselessly proclaim tourist traps
Tidally locked in the 1950s
An era no more innocent than before or since
The mockery apparent with even a modicum of history
Or taste
Later
The hills loom on that distant horizon
A startling apparition after so much space
The dark pines swallow all that sunlight
Black only in contrast to the scorched expanse below
But yes a contrast
Hiking the back side of Harney Peak
The attractions are subtle
And you know many were here
Long before you
A spiritual history gently makes itself known
At a clearing
Or among a vaguely geometric cluster of tall boulders
The pines enclosing it all
And you can understand why this was the last stand
These hills were defended as sacred
From those who held only gold and silver as sacred
And when even Crazy Horse couldn't defend them any longer
Voluntarily surrendering

The quiet warrior
Was asked to attend a meeting
But on arrival was taken to prison
Where he resisted and was killed by bayonet
His likeness never captured by photo or paint
Death by such trickery
Was not sufficient
And so a giant mountain carving of Crazy Horse
Is slowly chiseled
Desecrating one people's sacred space
Another people's national forest
And one man's memory
At the gate you are asked $18 to see this
Because the sculptor
Who is crazy with a small c
Wants this to be a monument to "free enterprise"
But has taken so long
Because of long timeouts for fundraising
While refusing government grants
That it is falling apart even though still half finished
A quintuple insult
A feat rare even for American capitalism
Not far away is Mount Rushmore
A feat of triumphalism and vacuity
That thumbs you in the eye
And you can only blink in amazement
That such arrogance could be mounted so proudly
All this and the other commercial attractions
So lacking in dignity but almost subtle in comparison
Lovingly promoted in the village of Keystone in the valley below
It seems no one lives there
Keystone exists solely to demonstrate humanity's triumph
Over nature and sense

How the hills must weep at night
Softened by erosion yet dramatic
An understated counterpoint to the Rockies
 From an orbital perch
You watch the weather move in from the west
The flat Earth curve away to the east
And you are where you are supposed to be
The pines follow you to the top
And it doesn't matter if lunch is good
The contradictions are left at a lower elevation
Only later do you wonder at the need
For any artificial stimulation
 From the time when the treaties were broken
And the mining began
Such a place
Is seen only as a profit center
And don't sniff at your ancestors
That is as true today
I wonder
What the biggest insult is

Lucille Lang Day

710 Ashbury, 1967
For Gene Anthony

The photographer hangs out on Haight Street,
entranced by youths in beads
and braless girls in lace and feathers
who weave flowers in their hair.
He smokes weed with his subjects
and taps his foot to the beat
of Jimi, Janis, and the Jefferson Airplane.

He has told his agent not to call him:
"No more dogs, flags, wine labels,
politicians, or corporate portraits."
In his office in New York
the agent paces. He's apoplectic,
so many clients waiting.
His guy in San Francisco is a flake—

lugging his camera bag up Ashbury,
where nothing is more important
than Jerry Garcia in his Uncle Sam hat
and Phil Lesh with a golf club.
The photographer rings the bell at 710,
tells the Dead where to stand,
and the world snaps into place.

Marty McConnell

Geometry of the Obvious

Betsy Ross is an overstuffed armchair,
torn spot in the cosmos, all exposed tacks
and threadbare, a given. *these colors
do run,* she says, lost in history's
junk room. *I wanted tree-light
sifting through lace, candle wax
warping on glass – or snow
with molasses patterns. but they
wanted geometry, those gods
of the obvious.* Betsy shifts
her square feet, the plush back
puffing with each sigh. *kicking
up dust with those boys was like
preaching to a wheelbarrow.*
where cushion meets arm,
a mouse tucks his collapsible
bones. Betsy Ross is an overstuffed
armchair, faux needlepoint tapestry
wanting just one more tongue, once more
the traffic of buggies, of boot-clad men
who come calling well before
the war begins, want a flag sewn
under which to lie.

Joanne Lowery

Saving Abe

Turning off the television documentary
when it gets to March, 1865, doesn't work:
in all the books he still dies
at the hand of a drunken madman,
the kind boarding houses are full of.
If not John, then Tom, Dick, or Harry.

Perhaps a different, shorter hat
with a lower profile would keep him
alive until fashion changed.
We could burn the newspapers
that cartooned him as a gorilla.
Mary might teach him to smile.

If he knew historians would always vote
him the greatest president,
he'd have better things to do
than go to the theater that night.
Stay home, sleep, become
a silver-haired grandfather.
Slip between sickness and assassination
safely, eloquently, interminably.
Free himself, along with the slaves.

Instead April comes and history happens.
He stays very dead.
People write biographies, mint pennies.
And still *if only* comes to mind,
denial the final form of praise.

Valerie Lawson

Don't Tread On Me

>"Same as it ever was"
>David Byrne

Bicentennial graduation remembered for "Spirit,"
our yearbook cover a tiger draped on a bold "76,"
one fat paw dangling off the edge.
In the first war of independence
my town flew a flag that said "Don't Tread On Me."
My high school was orange and black
not red, white, and blue. We longed
for revolution, wore our colors on our jeans,
cocked at the hip, sides slit to the knee,
bells stitched to the gap, guitar strap
edges sewed on the hem, American flags
slapped on our asses, psychedelic flowers
stitched around it. We were all future, no past,
ignored red and white stripes and went for blue field.

The stars, man, they shone bright,
we owned every constellation.
This was the Age of Aquarius,
this was our country: America .
We loved it, the way you love your Daddy
when he unstraps his belt and lays one on;
the way you love the surgery that saved your life
but took the legs shattered when you stepped on a land mine.

Our stars were shot from the sky.
Tiny points of light shine
but we can't connect the dots.
Other stars have punched
new constellations: industrial warfare,
IED, RPG, clean up contracts,
"Go Blackwater, keep on rollin'"
it's a knock knock joke: who's there;
"one if by jungle, two if by desert."

We were orange and black, blue and gold,
green and crimson; we were all red, white, and blue.
Colors don't run, they get sucked into mud,
can't make headway on shifting sand,
red bleeds and bleeds into the white stripe of peace.
We screamed when fathers and brothers went to war,
shrug our shoulders as we send our daughters and sons.

In front of City Hall, an untended flag pivots
on a single grommet, winds round itself,
hangs like a club in a corner.
I don't want to burn that flag,
don't want to stitch it to my ass either.
I'm not interested in your lies,
so don't wave it in my face,
don't tell me you're making our world safe.
We were raised on "ask not" and "dreams"
they were gunned down. They took our Kennedys
and our King, gunned us down at Kent State.
They didn't get us all and we're not done yet.
Tiger stripes are camouflage, don't be fooled
by hooded eyes and slack paws.
We've still got a pen and the freedom to speak.
We may go grey, we may fade to black,
but we're not about to disappear,
if we keep shouting, eventually someone will hear.

Anne Brudevold

Seascape

Dunes fold into a hollow space
where summer slips autumn into the rose's hips
oh, the spent roses on the cliff's high space
gathered in the bay, the army of ships

summer slips autumn into roses' hips
the lighthouse arcs a sky embrace
far in the horizon, the army of ships
etched forever his living face

the lighthouse arcs a sky embrace
she closes her eyes, under her lids
etched forever his living face
his legs, his arms, all his ribs

she closes her eyes, under her lids
she sees him in Tet, a murderous place
his legs, his arms, all his ribs
his shape is vague across a great space

she sees him in Tet, a murderous place
he kills men, slams casket lids
his shape is vague across a great space
she sees him explode, she sees him dead.

He loses an arm and then a face
the woman rocks an empty crib
no baby will know his arms, no trace
no man should give his life for war's empty fib

the woman rocks an empty crib
dunes fold into a hollow space
no man should give his life for war's empty fib
oh, the spent roses on the cliff's high face.

Jennifer Wallace

A Slow-filling Cloud

Ft. McHenry splits the river, the brown river
that drains the city. The harbor,

a garden of booms and girders,
weekend boaters, and rafts of debris.

History animates the ramparts
where privates stacked the 18-pound balls
and surgeons wrapped the fallen in cloth.

What blows through the marsh,
like wind? Through the trees.

Tourists breathe their citizenship.
We breathe

with the sparrow, the widow,
her 15-star banner. With her neighbors

the night of the battle. Who tripped on the cobbles
in flight from attackers who march with us now
breathing a desert - its own forts and rivers.

What inspiration: this river that flows
from faraway farms where blue and grey brothers

shot at each other. Those ruddy waters
still rise to rain on this fort and the oceans beyond.

We breathe a republic of rockets and rivers,
of tourists, of flotsam, of flags and of song.

Like a thread, like a knot,
a map that ascends with the river's mild vapors.

This is history. A slow-filling cloud.

Gretchen Fletcher

Too Blue Skies

I've come to fear too blue skies.
Each time it was the same:
the sky squeezed out of a tube
labeled "cerulean," (you know, that really
really blue) that formed a painted backdrop
for the dramas we watched.

    I

The sky the color of Texas Bluebonnets
set off that fuchsia suit she would insist on
wearing all day even splattered with his blood
as red as the armful of roses she wouldn't put down –
the only visible cloud that day,
a small puff of smoke that rose
from behind an umbrella on a grassy knoll.

    II

No clouds in that cold sky either, the one
as blue as the Atlantic their daughter was to soar over,
a pristine canvas for a surreal picture
like one of those slo-mo films of blossoms
opening, unfurling petals and tendrils.
Like a climbing vine it played out above
faces trying to register both pride and shock –
till the parents were ushered kindly off the stands.

    III

We should have known by then to beware
of too blue skies, but one more drama
played out against a sky of unnatural clarity
in a city so often shrouded in pollution.
Orange flames in that blue sky,

opposites on the color wheel,
created a jarring scene
of what looked like some giant fall
Chrysanthemums blooming on two thick stems.

David Wolf

Maneuvers

I grew up in a house with seven TVs.
I liked it when the heroes got it in the end.

When my grandmother came to sit
she'd line up three sets in a row
and watch three different channels at once.
I'd kneel beside her
and slap the fat on her arms for fun.

Summers when the reruns couldn't hold us,
my brother and I would hunt each other down
in the woods behind our house,
armed with the latest toy weapons
or Dad's .45 without the clip.

If you got hit you were dead for 60 seconds.

One night I didn't get up.
My brother never returned to finish me off.
I lay there watching the darkness close down the view,
thinking of the release that always fell
over the unshaven faces of heroes
dying in the arms of some full-figured woman.
I lay there letting the mosquitoes fill with blood,
trying to slow my heart to starve them off.
I lay there in the swell of the locusts,
trying to make it real.

Bruce Weber

Toy Soldiers

my daddy bought me a thousand toy soldiers
and i play war whenever i'm alone.
sometimes in the early morning light
i arrange them in infantries
along the ridges and valleys of my bed sheets
sending hundreds to their death
in the cauldron of wrinkles and folds.
someday i'm going to shoot my enemies
that's what my daddy tells me.
now me and my buddies
go rat a tat tat
and somebody falls down
but they're only fooling.
anyway i prefer playing with my soldiers.
sometimes i fight the battle of gettysburg
over and over on my bed
arranging the blanket
like devil's den
or cemetery ridge.
i get a lot of satisfaction
watching rebels fall.
this is more fun
than dancing with all those silly girls.
someday i'll be smarter than everybody
and have a big farm in pennsylvania
and hire some immigrants
to re-enact the battle of iwo jima.
but now i play alone
with my soldiers
while nobody's looking
in the privacy of my room . . .
i can kill anyone.

Artie Moffa

Stereo Sun

Democracy does not exist
In all locations. Witness that
Rough soccer field. We hundreds sat
Incarcerated out-of-doors.
We sat. We weren't allowed to stand.
Camp Tockwaugh. August. Maryland.
The guards were ancient. College kids.
(I knew enough to know I lacked
Perspective.) Although, looking back
They still seem old. Our counselors,
They"d brought chairs. From the tennis courts
They sat in judgment, wearing shorts.
The sun absolved the dew from blade and leaf.
The day grew warm. Our numbers hid a thief.
"A stereo is missing," said
The Council chief. "A new CD
Cassette deck. It's a JVC.
It disappeared last night" he glanced,
"From cabin F, in Iroquois."
We all looked at the red-haired boy.
"This shouldn't take too long," the chief
Continued, "but it all depends
On you guys. Everybody spends
The day outside. We'll sit and wait.
Somebody has this stereo.
Just own up and we'll let you go."
And then came the predictable response.
Indignant silence mumbled up at once.
What happened next took guts. A rich
And heavy camper raised his hand.
Our voices fell. He made to stand.
"I have to take my insulin
At ten." (The time was quarter to.)

We saw they hadn't thought this through.
Of course, there was a sudden plague
Of hypochondria. Complaints
Were sunstroke, heartburn, rashes, sprains
And diarrhea. That was real.
We'd all been shitting mud all week
From drinking filtered Chesapeake.

Our counselors conferred. I heard them curse.
They organized small groups to see the nurse.
We envied those who left, as if
They'd have adventures. But they'd soon
Return. The sun cried "Whee!" at noon
And braced for its decent. The thief
Was silent. We got paper cups
Of water and we drank them up.
They told us not to talk. We did.
Clandestine conversations came
And went. They'd silence us by name:
"No talking, Jill!" So Jill shut up
For maybe thirty seconds, tops.
Our counselors made lousy cops.
And after all, what more could they have done?
Give harsher punishment? There wasn't one.
Some people don't believe me. They
Insist it's not American.
"But weren't the parents angry when
They heard?" I think they miss the point
Of camp. Our parents sent us there
For structure, sunshine, and fresh air.
They paid to have us supervised.
Mom baked cookies, dad sent notes.
They'd spend their two weeks sailing boats
Or catching up with college friends.
They'd play golf, they'd make love, they'd read.
I'm sure some smoked a little weed

And after fourteen nights of barbecues
They'd take us home, and shrug off bad reviews.
A few rows up from me I saw
Melissa. She was twelve. We'd met
That week. I hadn't kissed her yet,
But we had danced, and I had hopes.
She shaved her legs. Her hair was blonde.
We'd shared a S'more by Mohawk pond.

I pitied Red-haired Paul. This was
His fault. In part. Not really. Still,
It was his stereo. Until
The thief stood up, we'd just blame Paul.
Why bring that stereo to camp?
I'd brought a tiny fan and lamp.
He sat with them, a ruined tattletale.
We sat and hated him. We sat in jail.
I have some more perspective now.
Camp Tockwaugh isn't cheap. You pay
A pretty penny for your stay.
You have to judge it as a camp.
We slept in cabins, not in tents.
They packed our days with fun events.
I wasn't rich. My parents drove
A Ford. Able cars. Nothing great.
I didn't understand the state
Of wealth that is America.
Most families don't have new cars,
Yet I felt poor from inside ours.
No politician thinks herself extreme.
No man is rich by measure of his dream.
I grew impatient, so I dared
To speak. "This is ridiculous!
You really think that one of us
Would steal something as big as that?
It's huge! Nobody has the space
To hide it from his cabin-mates."

I've never been so honest or
So brave. At least, not publicly.
Melissa noticed. As for me,
My knees grew weak and I sat down.
The Council Chief, no seasoned judge
When faced with doubt, refused to budge.
The seconds stretched back out to normal length
And I calmed down. My knees regained their strength.

We felt at least a hundred times
Our age. Our asses were asleep.
Our necks were burnt. Some couldn't keep
From laughing. Giggles rippled out
In simple rings. Boys twisted grass,
Girls braided hair. Our eyes were glass.
The smallest trifle was a prized
Possession. One green tennis ball
Became a game for hundreds. All
Our paper went for airplanes. Then
The younger boys discovered weeds
Which made good blowguns. They shot seeds.
We older boys just sneered and said, "How cute."
We watched them for a time, then followed suit.
I was well-to-do, but they
Were wealthy. We would meet again
In college. Haverford and Penn
Were full of Tockwaugh kids. The kind
From New York or Connecticut.
They went down South for camp. That's it.
And Maryland is South the way that
Dublin is in Europe. Yes,
It's true in maps and books, unless
You've been there, and discovered you
Can speak and listen. Maryland
Is swampy, mixing mud and sand.
It sits uncomfortably in-between
Two territories. Median and mean.

We slumped and slept the afternoon
Away. Melissa's face was red.
We all got burns. Somebody said,
"I think I'm gonna faint!" We got
More water. Warm. It missed the spot.
I don't think, in a million years,
The counselors expected it
Would last this long. They thought we'd sit
For twenty minutes. After that
A tattletale would. Or else the thief
Would stand. They thought this would be brief.
They dealt us punishment three-hundred times
Too big to fit one theft, the least of crimes.

We finally were saved by that
Which tortured us. The sky turned gray
And thunder rolled across the bay.
We all prayed for a hurricane.
Three-hundred campers held out palms
For cooling raindrops, heaven's balms.
We knew that we had won. That is
We campers. We had forced a draw.
It may have been against the law
To keep us in the sun, but in
A thunderstorm? That's homicide!
They had to let us back inside.
A tree split into flames. We campers fled
Inside the dining hall, where we were fed.
By Thursday, we'd forgotten all
About it. We had boats to sail,
And songs to sing, and girls to fail
To kiss. Melissa hurt her leg
While water-skiing. At the dance
She sat apart. I missed my chance.
On Saturday our parents came.
My huge and heavy laundry sack

Went in the trunk. Way in the back.
My parents did the rest. I said
Goodbye to friends I would not miss.
There's nothing left to tell, save this:
I've kept it to this day. It still sounds great.
Worth every penny paid, and worth the wait.

Stephen Lindow

Dryer

The domestic bathyscaph
called me under our basement steps
with plunking and shuddering.

        Hotpoint. Energy Saver.   Three-Wire.

        I watched static-breath freckling
        my corduroy long sleeves and socks,
        round and round into magnetic kink.
        I scooped the soft remains of
        Sasquatch with my hand from an alcove

        and climbed within for a warm spin.
        It was a round elevator from the Gateway Arch.
        I sat on a steel fin, and prepared to be swallowed
        up the leg of a great grey
        dinosaur who drank from the Mississippi.

        A klaxon snared the soft knit night,
        or was it Mom yanking me out of there.
        I never fell for its dark song loop again.

        An underground Ferris Wheel it was not.
        My seven-year-old body:

        Burnt. Dizzy.   All night.

Lewis Gardner

A Gift from Great-Aunt Prudence

In the early days of liberated consciousness–
1967, to be exact–
I was cashier in a shop of imported
goods. One cargo included hand-carved
wooden sculptures from Taiwan
of a hand with upraised middle finger.

This wasn't the plastic gewgaw
you later saw everywhere, but something
no doubt crafted by carvers with generations
of tradition behind them, who assumed
this strange object had religious
significance for Americans.

One night a little old lady –
since this was Boston , a very Bostonian
old lady – brought six of them
to my counter. "Such lovely ring holders,"
she said to me, "just the thing
for my grandnephews this Christmas."

So early in the days of liberated
consciousness – and in Boston besides –
I didn't know how to tell an old lady
that these items were neither ring holders
nor suitable gifts for her grandnephews.
So I rang them up and bagged them.

Besides, I really enjoyed imagining
Christmas morning in Cambridge, Duxbury,
Manchester-by-the-Sea,
as one by one they would open
neatly wrapped packages sent
with love by Great-Aunt Prudence.

Bob Hoeppner

Picnic

A burger was so infatuated,
meaning, not full of fat, though it was,
but it was so hot for a hot dog
that it painted a picture of it
in ketchup and mustard on its own flesh.
It was gonna keep its love secret
but someone said, hey burger, lift up your bun!
And there it was, the picture of the hot dog
blurry, but still recognizable.
The hot dog felt so embarrassed,
it didn't know what it would tell the relish
that hugged it, but whose grip was slipping.
The hot dog waited, thinking, then dumped
the relish and ran bun-less into the waiting steam
of the burger. They lay together as time bit their bodies
away. They left a legacy of crumbs that led back to the
    relish.
And the relish? It's living happily ever after on a plastic plate
that was so lonely and now gives unconditional love.

Gretchen Fletcher

Ah, Yes, the Fourth

Oh, say, it's that day when dads throw pop flies to sons
while girls' collections of minnows swirl ever slower
in Styrofoam cups of warming water till someone knocks
 them over,
and teenage boys line up illegal arsenals bought from local
 legend, Sparky,
while moms, wondering how long the potato salad can sit
 out,
chase pesky flies from patriotic-colored pies – blueberry and
 strawberry.
The watermelon floats in chunks of ice, its seeds soon to be
 spat across the grass
toward folding chairs that wobble, half their legs sunk in the
 sod.
And everybody prays away the rain as fireflies flicker
 previews of the lights to come,
and, beyond slammed screen doors, VCR's record
 Tchaikovsky in Boston
with all those bells and cannons, and somebody says
 something about freedom,
and cherry bombs and bottle rockets make everybody feel
 proud to be American.

Madeline Artenberg

Chosen Seats

His nose was a curved pot-bellied stove.
Grandpa was a six-foot two episode
in my land of five footers.

We'd quietly walk along Bay Parkway, stopping when
I pointed at jujubes or *Superman* comic books.
When he caught my finger in the foam half
of his evening's *Rheingold*,
he poured me my own in a jelly glass.
It's good, it's medicine, he said.

Grandpa rode his wooden rocking chair
in front of the bedroom window
like an Orthodox Jewish cowboy.
Traditional leather straps wrapped around his arms
fluttered as if fringes on a suede jacket,
greying sacred cloth showed below his vested sweaters.

I'd perch backwards in the window seat between
the frame and the bowed grill rail,
watching him with the straps, the shawl, and reciting
from thick and thin tomes,
edges curled like appendages.

When I read out loud from library books,
he'd point to letters.
On the next visit to the candy store,
we bought a black and white notebook,
mottled like a cow's hide.
He practiced ABCs in capitals and lower case;
I could not break his habit of writing from right to left

Once he took me by the hand
down the Parkway to his synagogue,
up a staircase to the second floor,
filled only with women and girls.
Grandpa let go my hand and reappeared downstairs
among hundreds of men wearing caps like his,
swaying, praying, buzzing like bees.

He wet his fingertips to turn the page.
I leaned over the balcony screaming, *Grandpa,
don't leave me up here, I'm not like them —
I'm your English teacher, I'm your Rheingold girl.*

Ted Giovannini

For Nonna

She was the light
in my life.
As a child
I could imagine
nothing more important
than my great-grandmother.
Nonna would sit
as I carefully brushed her
lustrous, long, silver hair
while she shared her childhood
in Nizza, Savoia,
a parcel of land no longer part of Italia,
but now called Nice.
Her preteen years in the Alps
after the death of her own sweet mother,
with her stepmother,
and the adolescence in a small village
in the Tuscan foothills of the Apennies.
I listened as the brush stroked.
I heard her life have meaning in mine:
Where I came from,
where I was now,
how it was
to come to America.

Tony Brown

Where Do You Live?

It was my sister-in-law's idea, I swear,
to hire the origami artist for Martha's birthday party.
I expected the kids to be bored, but
Yumiko's fingers snared all of us
as they delicately spidered
upon the paper and
began to
mold life into three dimensions from two,
taking us through a door into
a place
where one can build without cutting anything,
without making a Slot B to hold a Tab A.

She said it takes great peace of mind to learn to do this well.
She told us that in Hiroshima once a year,
thousands of people fold small paper boats,
set each boat on a river with a candle inside,
and let them drift and burn for peace.

Where are you from? Are you from there?
I asked her.
She said, *I was from there once, but now I am from America.
Where are you from?*

I would have liked to tell Yumiko that I am from America, too,
but I fear that I am instead from a place were origami comes
  to die
in the hands of market forces that make culture and tradition
a source of party tricks.
I would have liked to tell her that I live all my time in
  America,

but the truth is, I live most of my time in the United States—
because here are two countries that exist simultaneously on
   one geography.
Here is the US of radio designed by the moneyed calculus
   of bleating repetition.
Here is the America of the gospel choir that shouts for
   splendor even as the mob burns their church around them.
This is the US of terrific missiles and cars as large as our
   shrinking sense of control.
This is the America of outsider art, free jazz, and mall
   mercies shown to the smallest and strangest of us.
This is the US of sweet plastic that has ignited and burned
   through all the easy answers,
the land of the fire that has begun to lick at the edges of the
   America of red sandstone, deep woods, wide rivers;
the America where we always remember that we are all
   descended from someone somewhere
who burned; the place where we care about those
who have been burned, are being burned,
where we pray we can be forgiven by those we have burned,
pray that we can all make ourselves whole
by making our common home among the folds and creases
of a single idea: that we created the US as a launching pad
   toward America,
and if we didn't like the footing it gave us, we could always
   change it.
But it did seem to me (after that one red second had passed)
that it was too much to ask a paper crane folded for
entertainment at a child's birthday party
to balance all this weight—
even though people come here all the time to balance their
   dreams on our old paper
and there are people in Japan who annually load the fate of
   the world onto burning paper boats—

so instead I told Yumiko,
I am from right here, too.
And at least for that moment,
it was true.

And soon enough, a dozen cranes
were on the table,
and Yumiko showed us how
a tug on the tail will set the wings in motion;
and the children were hushed
as they handled each one
and tried it for themselves;
and soon enough,
small, important flights were beginning
all around the backyard.

Michele Sackman

The Quilting Bee

Many years later, I run my hands over
This quilt from the family, the Missouri branch

Memories bubble up of that summer spent on the farm
Watching Grandma Bass assemble a quilt top with her
  dressmaking leftovers
Jackie and my gingham skirts lavender with cross-stitched
  border stars
Cousin Ellie's calico dress trimmed at the neck with rickrack
These small squares of cloth pieced and sewn onto a white
  cotton top
Creating memories in this colorful top of spring dresses

I remember riding in the back of Aunt Junes' pickup truck
With my cousins Larry, Sherry and the runt (called Ronnie
  by his Mom)
We teased and joked in the back, talked about noodling for
  fish at the pond
Grandma and June rode up in the front with the potato
  salad
Ignoring all of us and our squabbles

Grandma was bringing her new quilt top to the Wednesday
  quilting bee
A potluck lunch with lots of salads and strange canned
  seafood patties
An amazing array of Jello salads in reds, greens and yellows
Filled with fruits, nuts and vegetables
When we kids came in for lunch we ate ourselves silly

The women got back to their work and gossip
We were shooed outside to play tag under the trees
Hide and seek in the nearby woods
We explored the cornfields now higher than our heads
Before we knew it, afternoon was done
Called back to the house, we piled into the truck
Grandma and June with the new quilt
Meticulously stitched by twelve women
An effort of many hands, an American tradition
Common life family history
Small moments writ in a creation of beauty
One of a kind, usable art

Kim Roberts

"Lyda E. Pinkham's Vegetable Compound"

      A nostrum and medicament
pleasant to the taste and efficacious
      in curing female weaknesses
including falling of the womb,
      painful menstruation,
and inflammation of the generative organs.

      A tablespoon every four hours
is regarded as second to no other remedy
      for relieving the delicacy
and suffering peculiar to our sex.
      Safe! Sure! Speedy!
Never known to fail.

      You will feel like a new woman,
freed from overwrought nerves,
      hysteria, violent beating of the heart,
muscular spasms, and extravagance.
      Price $1.00 per bottle.
Shake before using.

Wendy Vardaman

Roosters and Hens

At bedtime Mother told us about growing
up on her grandparents' farm, chasing chickens
across the yard, peering into their dark home.
How Grandfather got the axe when Grandmother

wanted a bird for the stew pot and the time
she saw a crestfallen rooster on his feet,
the head cut off. Terrified at eight or nine,
she ran blindly in the other direction,

only to have him turn and chase her toward
the fence where she set one new white-sandaled foot
on a fresh cow pie. Grandfather roared, doubling
over his blade while she cried, hopped up and down,

tried to shake the shit from her toes. The sandals
were never the same, despite Grandmother's "Good
as new" when she finished scratching at the straps.
Mother said she could never wear open shoes

again, and left the farm, still a girl, to work
in the city, marry my father, and buy
painted porcelain roosters that collected
like dust over reminisced childhood. They hung

from avocado walls, crowed at the sink, caught
grease and dirt near the stove, presided over
the orange island counter top where my dad
also liked to roost with cigarettes and beers

he never got himself but called for from his
bar-stool perch, demanding that we leave our ranch
house coops, yelling no matter how long it took,
Mother clucking, "Wouldn't hurt you two to help."

Thomas D. Jones

A Bagger's Life

Plastic or paper?
Double, single, or triple bag?
Don't want it to break; groceries
spill and roll on the floor.
"Double bag only with paper,
careful not to squash the fruit!"
the little old lady
scolds the uniformed bagger.
"Only with paper?" he thinks, poems
scribbled in blue on the sides,
each line set into place.

The poet, the bagger, stops for a break,
takes a sandwich from the fridge
and paper from a satchel.
He writes only about what he knows:
how butchers wrap fresh meat,
careful to touch it with gloves
and wrap the plastic around it.
How produce clerks make salad,
Mix lettuce, peppers, tomatoes, and olives.
How pharmacists grab pills from the shelf,
Count each one with dainty care,
Pour the correct dose in the bottle.
How customer service develops pictures,
Stacks negatives and positives together.
How bakers display the newest cakes,
The frosting newly spread on the top.

His coworkers think him crazy
to write down dreams between stocking shelves,
to leave little notes in the lettuce patch,
to write on the lids, containers, and cans
of soup, assorted nuts, and coffee grounds.
They catch him writing on huge boxes
Of paper towels before they go in a truck.
The poem, like bagging or stocking shelves,
Requires focus to get it right:
the cans, the fruit, the frozen dinners,
each one carefully chosen to fit on the shelf,
each handled with care in the bag.

He stares at the customers, grocery laden,
Their world apart from his,
Each item inching closer and closer,
the pile larger and larger, as if growing in size.
He grabs each thing off the conveyor
And thinks of a line for his newest poem,
Of all the poems he's read,
Along with the lettuce, ground beef, chicken breasts,
And pork rinds ever bagged. Each one vanishes
Into the bag, but later he pulls out his pad
And records them on paper.

The conveyor moves like a treadmill,
Endless with each new customer.
The food people did not kill,
And the vegetables they did not grow
Continue mindless toward his hands,
The rhythm hurried with no breath or relief.
The poet turns to the other baggers
Who throw each item in the bag
Without a thought or concern. He thinks
About going home, about the poems yet to write.

Laura Lee Washburn

S & H Green Stamps

I.
My mom had a three-legged stool,
needlepoint on top, ivory with pink flowers,
and a little handle sticking out
with a leather strap, as though
it should be hung legs out from a wall.
The stool taught us balance
when we reached to high shelves.
My mother found it beautiful.
Granny Johnson bought it for her
with S & H Green Stamps.

II.
I still think of them somehow
as dimes, green tickets printed
with red "tens." You
could find them loose
in the silverware drawer
alongside the plastic tray
or discover stray stamps
next to the rubber bottle caps,
the copper jar opener, the extra key
or any of a dozen things now
fallen out of our lives.

III.
I conspired one year with my cousin
to gather all the books
my mother had saved, the extra stamps
left here and there, some
from my grandparents and an aunt,
and to "buy" her the new dishes
she'd wanted from the store,

that ironstone decorated with the blue
Pennsylvania Dutch flower.
We felt proud and adult buying dishes
with stamps Mom probably didn't want to lick.
I shouldn't mention this: years later
my dad's second wife brought her own
set of the same dishes into marriage.

IV.
The S & H Green Stamp dispenser
was attached to a post by the register.
I turned it by clicks, a stamp a dollar,
and no more. They were falling out
of fashion and frequently refused.
The dispenser was red. The stamps
stuck out in a satisfying train
signifying stacked brown bags of groceries.

I didn't know how much the world
could change back then. I was paid
in cash, and I walked through the store
to the savings and loan's adjoining window
and made my deposits. Even tonight
I wasn't thinking of the world until surprised
by those stamps. I would like to have
twenty books of them, bound
by a red newspaper rubber band.
I would like my good cousin to drive
me to the redemption center. I want to walk
up and down the shelved aisles,
seeing everything America can offer
neat, clean, and domestic. All those licked
stamps, the saver books—I'll never be so rich again.

Lewis Gardner

Pennies

It used to be good luck to find one.
Some were steel, some had the profile
of an Indian. Boys pressed collections
into the round slots of blue folders.
Now they are trash, a nuisance,
stored in cans and jars
till they're rolled for the bank.

Listen, kids: this copper-colored disk
could transform a summer morning,
redeemed at the corner store
for a paper strip of candy dots
in four colors, a wax bottle
of grape or cherry syrup, or a crunchy,
peanut-flavored Mary Jane.

Ryk McIntyre

Penny Candy Store

A child's first glimpse of an infinity I could understand,
all the clear nights counting stars never prepared me
for every color, hundreds of smells, a thousand promises
of sweet heaven. My meager allowance had power

I never imagined! I could choose and choose and still
have coins left in my hand, hot dollars burning holes
clear through my pockets, calling out to my heart
by way of eager stomach. I knew the danger of want.

The greeting bell on the door was bright and sharp like
crossing a magical portal should be. I knew the difference
between here and there: "here" was every place I had to be
but didn't want to be; "there" smelled of sugar and magic,

of chocolate and bull's eyes, root-beer barrels and fireballs.
There were special conditions to recognize and place:
a wooden floor worn comfortable and smooth, windows
like scrying glass you had to dream through. I'd promise

myself I wouldn't cry, but I cried every time. No place for
plastic packaging, out of reach over my sweaty head,
this was a temple for bare hands and metal scoops
to hunt and circle, dive and plunge, then rise up, full to

bursting, weight of treasure reverently placed in paper bags
that snapped open to attention, like it expected my arrival.
Kinetic with excitement, fabulously rich with sugar,
forgetting schoolwork, invulnerable for an afternoon,
   far away from here.

Jeff Poniewaz

Turkey in the Straw
for Charles Ives

Today is the day of the bird
Ben Franklin preferred
to the eagle. How could he know
they'd name dime stores after him?
How could he know the America
he autographed the Independence of
would gobble the globe
and regurgitate on the moon?
Every time I go to buy groceries,
I get a free garbage bag
to carry them home in.
And so on this day
of national cornucopia
let us gather by the river
in William Duffy's barn
to hear Ives' Fourth Symphony
conducted by the original siamese twins,
Chang and Eng, and digest this thought
with heads bowed before digging in:
Since science is constantly discovering
deleterious properties in the foods we partake,
it would seem we are in the gradual process
of poisoning ourselves.
Half-eaten drumstick in hand,
I warn the human race as Death's teeth
close on me: "It's the food...GASP...
don't eat it...GURGLE...it will kill you
from the inside like a Trojan horse...
AARRGH...if only you can figure out
how not to eat without starving,
you will never die!"

Hal Sirowitz

Where the Buffalo Went

'buffalo bill is defunct,'
ee cummings wrote,
but that was before they
marketed bison burgers.
Instead of selling tickets
to his 'Wild West
Traveling Show,'
he's helping to sell
burgers by having
his picture on the cover
of one of the more
popular brands, proving
that an American icon
might die, but that
doesn't diminish
his selling power.

Kim Roberts

New Haven

You might see an elephant
plowing a wheat field, some mild evening
in early Fall,
        just past New Haven,

timed for the evening commute.
If you press your face against
the window-glass, you can see
        in the distance

P.T. Barnum's mansion, Iranistan,
iced like a confection—
with turrets and gilded domes
        and four stories

of wrap-around porches
dripping with carved scrollwork.
The Old Humbug's not at home.
        He's off to Europe

with his pretty young niece
to buy us something new—
dog-faced boys, bearded ladies,
        midgets, Siamese twins.

Helen Ruggieri

The Last Performing Wallendas

from a newspaper account of Angel & Steve Wallenda's final performance in Galeton, PA.

At 21 Angel has lung cancer
the doctors say surgery is risky
and she would have to breathe
using oxygen tanks
as if she lived in an underwater kingdom
under a heavier gravity.
Angel will perform tonight
her farewell appearance with
her husband, Steven, a Viet Nam vet
who wants to call attention to the MIA's,
to bring those missing home.

Angel and Steve will walk on air
more graceful than mere humans;
they will float above the crowd
lighter than gossamer,
brighter than spangles.
They will walk above us
as if they were a lost species.
as if their DNA changed
and made them into the future
their cells mutating,

the world below all pale and noisy.
In the lighted center ring
they are what was intended.
There are so many causes;
they will find what they are missing.

Elizabeth Kerlikowske

Jane's Shadow Family

Mother buys a muumuu splattered with
gardenias to commemorate Hawaii 's
statehood and wears it for years on the couch spattered
with muted leaf forms from a temperate zone,
Eden in the living room, TV dinners
in aluminum trays and Tang. Astronauts
drink Tang. Her pearls sweat in the crease
of her neck. She's done hiding in the back yard
to smoke. We pray she won't be room mother.

Father is part time: TV repairman,
lawn care; someone else's name sewn on
the shirt he got for free. Dick calls him
LaVonne behind his back. He scrounged our bikes
from Thursday's trash pick-up in a nice neighborhood.
Fridays there's a poker game; I try to find
a sleep-over. Saturday the rugs smell like beer.

Dick runs with the AV boys who skip
school and smoke dope at Mr. Fables. Dick's
a graphic artist; our parents think we have
all As. Dick's Trojans roll under his mattress.

I press myself into a locker when the Jets sweep
the halls in their cardigan sets and page boys.
Generosity's a crime in the cafeteria
and Father is too proud for free lunch.
I sometimes throw away my pencil to steal
an apple from the trash.

Sally still doesn't talk but drags terrible Tim
her bear everywhere. Her hair's grown back blonder
curlier but still no one invites her to their parties;
she wasn't the only one with lice, a Brownie
on probation.

This Thanksgiving, the charity turkey knocked
at our door, so you can imagine Mom and Pop's
surprise when Scott Foresman calls to say he wants
to write a book based on our lives.

Lenore Weiss

Ode to Emeril

While the stock market crumbled
and the dot.com bust
burst a generation's dream to retire at 40
while everything was slip sliding away
and corporate greed became a thing of mythology
and all the whistle-blowers were women,
who was by my side?

Emeril Lagasse from FoodTV NetWork—
cute white apron tied around your middle-aged paunch,
more like an egg soufflé with Bam!
a dash of Essence.

Throughout 9/11 and beyond
I channel-surfed to you,
watched onion, celery, and pepper—
holy trinity of New Orleans cooking—
become translucent.

You showed me the love,
how to make my food taste better,
if a piece of chocolate cake crumbled,
to disguise the breach—

I was with you for the crowning of Miss Crustacean
then back on CNN, counted the death toll—
at commercial break, hoped to God
you'd never eaten at McDonald's,
and even if you *had* visited the golden arches,
knew you'd cut out early to dice garlic,
make some kick-ass vodka sauce,
cook your own damn hamburger

reminding me
although the world
is a paean to war,
we can make each other
happy, happy, happy

with a shivering mousse,
a warm tureen

So whenever you decide
to throw an international pot luck
televised from NYC
Emeril, do me a favor—
invite me.

Suzanne Frank

On Losing Faith

> "Captain Stormfield found on arriving in Heaven that
> angel wings are mostly ornamental and not to fly with."
>
> —Mark Twain

Elvis wore a corset when he played Cobol Hall.
A sequined tube of macho wiping sweat

on silk scarves, he hurled them on the down
beat to swooning women tearing at their

beehive hair. That's where I lost my faith--
Detroit in '69, the year X meant Malcolm

and Amerika was spelled with a K, when
the Lady was easy, heavy arms holding

anyone for the night. Now the sky blooms red
over Bethlehem Steel and the guy on the next

blanket sings a Miller beer jingle, lights his
sparkler on a cigarette, slaps at mosquitoes.

Give me your huddled masses and I'll put
them to work pulling tight the strings on

the King's girdle, one foot against his back
as he grips the chair, yearning to breathe free.

David Lawton

Johnny Cash

Out of a stark landscape
Amongst the cotton leaves there grew
An apostle of the human experience
Of sin and redemption
Bad faith and gospel truth
Sourmash and bennies
And the rest that flesh is heir to
Hewn on his weathered face with grace
A voice like black strap molasses
That could keen like his Scots Irish kinfolk
Or screech like the rebel yell at Gettysburg
Plucking and slapping out a crude engine of rhythm
To take us through the darkness and into the light
From store bought radios and TV tubes
He brought the dirt poor with the dirt floor
The ragged old flag and the pompadour
The *Louisiana Hayride* and the convict's cell door
All cloaked in a simple suit of black–

The love he found redeemeth
He abideth in the sweet by-and-by.

Julia Gordon-Bramer

Viva Las Vegas

Driving weightless on Southwestern moonscape
Hypnotized by broken yellow lines of long
Nevada desert highways
Sun sinks before us; this indebted servant. Darkness sets
in. Glowing Vegas is fifty miles away and,
to be cliché because we're here:
a picture says a thousand words.
We pull in toward town around
midnight, the city exploded in light.
This is a town on purpose. Created
for no other
reason than fun

The ground hurts to stand on
In hateful bright day
zoysia lawns brown from brutality
of summer golden
dirt showing through the bald patches
like scalp on a gambling man's thinning
hair. The blue is clear with whispers
of clouds gathering in groups, streaked across
they carry intention of getting
somewhere, conspiring to create some
sort of system later. In the distance
rusty red mountains erupt
defying sensible gravity that perpetually
holds the rest of us down
Rising out from hard ground
mounds of sifted cocoa powder
Cut by long-gone ice; refuse
to conform

Clusters of cottages crawl
away from casinos and roads, from McCarran
Air and into the foothills
They climb the base as far as they can
without tumbling in the guilty weight
of losers back to try again
Shame, heat, dryness, greed
The world is governed by a kind
of cruelty. The best you can hope for
is chance. It's what we make
of our lucky breaks
They know this in Vegas

Mountain range open fissures and sore
spots of red clay. There's no more green
in the wallet. Wrinkles, gashes, the ravages
of time walk too; encase the neon birthday cake
Heaps of rocky fat frosting mount the edges of town
Tall, even-spaced palms along
the boulevard like too many
candles with tops bursting leafy fans of flame
It feels
like too much caffeine worn –
down, jittery, shaking from the on
switch stuck the volume too high, too long
You long
for a field, a quiet meadow
where there
is no such thing
as luck.

David Lee Summers

Racing Amtrak

Heading nor'east out of Las Vegas,
New Mexico, I look to my left and
I'm startled to see the Flying Dutchman
on rails – really the northbound Amtrak –
but hailing from the town where my
late father worked on locomotives
so many years ago.

As I continue northward, I look over
my shoulder and see that the train is
keeping pace with me. Easing my
foot off the gas, I fall back, letting
the train pull ahead a little. Pushing
on the accelerator again and we're
running neck and neck.

The railway and the highway converge and
tears come unbidden. Seeing the passengers,
I reach out, as though to touch them.
My effort is as futile as capturing the
memory of something yet to come.
The train slows at Old Fort Union.
The ghosts are home.

Sarah Getty

Rocks, Utah

Colors of flesh and blood—pink, tan, white, brown, red,
  vein-blue—
but fleshless, hard and dry as bone. Tumbled, heaped, layered,
rising sheer and slick from rubble, poking the sky like giants.

Old. Old. The same old thoughts, "All that time
without us." "We are but midges." But in a synapse-flash,
pride prods us to outdo them. The layers all have names,

but they don't even know it. Human beings named them;
a man imagined the great tongue of Mexico's gulf stretched
clear to Canada. Eons it licked the shores of Colorado,

California, laid down layer after layer. A man, a midge
like us, saw in his mind the layers lifting, tilting, explained
the sea shells topping the sandstone towers. Midges with
  brains,

we memorize the names: Kayenta, Wingate, Navajo, Chinle.
We play Spot the Layer as we hum west along Rt. 70
at 80 m.p.h. The Chinle is easy—it looks like turquoise.

The Navajo is brown, above the Chinle. Below the Chinle,
the Wingate is also brown. Unless that's the Moenkope.
Unless this is where the Moenkope's missing, because the sea

retreated for a while. Or maybe that brown stripe is the "red-
brown Kayenta, harder than the Wingate." We decide to just
enjoy the rocks. In all this time, they've never once admired

one another. Only we, the midges, have that power. And this:
soft, wet, mortal, we can mate. Tonight we'll do it again
in the Wingate Room at Castle Valley B&B. Years and years

too late to procreate, we still can do the dance, hard-wired
to create the next day's midges. Afterwards we'll lie there,
flat, happy, smelling of salt. All night, out on the black ridge,

Castle Rock alone under the moon while we keep breathing.
Come morning, we'll rouse to coffee and pancakes on the
 porch,
bird-song, dewdrops, and six deer nibbling the lawn along
the creek. Up on the ridge, Castle Rock alone under the sun.

Victoria Muñoz

Fresco From Summer

Driving through Farm Town, USA,
I see miles of corn and flat lands.
Farm stands sell carved wood keepsakes from Thailand.
Pies sold by ladies dressed in prairie dresses, the
men wore jeans. The sign in front read,
"Fresh fruit and vegetables today, even if it rains."

As the sun fades, flashes of light
pass between corn rows in a sweeping view
through back roads of Pennsylvania.

A corner of the world calls out with commotion.
Crowded front porches echo academia through midnight.
Streets breathe heavy with religion; crosses
stand out loud in headlights.

Determined horse and buggy silhouettes
lead the fifteen bicyclists
glowing in the dark of
white shirts, black pants
reflected from flashing lights of Rosie's diner:
"Home Cooked Amish."

I settle in for the night.

Bill MacMillan

Fayetteville to Memphis

his truck remembers the back-roads of Arkansas
like your momma remembers the gospel songs of her youth
Glory Glory
and he will be in Memphis by morning

movement is a placebo
false relief and no amount of coffee and aspirin is gonna fix
  this

Flo is a metaphor
she is alive in every diner between Louisville and Little
  Rock
only she doesn't have a beehive hairdo or chewing gum
and her name's not really Flo
but this is irrelevant to the story
some details are more important than others

what is relevant is the truck
every great departure needs the appropriate vehicle

The truck is American
like Mom
apple pie
heartbreak
he drives through Hope like a punch line
off color and poorly timed
his life has always been a series of double meanings
he will notice no ironies until it is too late

later, he will tell friends that perhaps he should have
traveled north instead
passed through Carthage and been released

like him, kudzu is not native to the south
it was intended to stop erosion
the road to hell will be paved with it

like kudzu, even if you poison his roots
he will continue to spread farther
settle in elsewhere

sunrise is an insult if you have to drive into it
it will make you long for the Tao of 3 a.m.
night is the absence of light
the sound of one hand clapping
while the other holds the wheel

his truck remembers the redundancy of roads
warmer breezes and frustrated feet
pushing peddles for no other reason than they could

his truck remembers oil and asphalt
and therefore understands
how things can change dramatically over time

his truck understands that motion
has nothing to do with movement

Memphis is an irony
a city ruled by a missing sovereign
in the and of plenty
we insist on letting ghosts guide our way

the king is dead
long live the king

Linda O'Connell

Wanderlust

Spring intoxicates me with memories of a bygone era
When every day was a childish adventure for Dad,
And he ran with wanderlust
When the winds spoke to his Native American soul.
I was along for the ride.

Snake-like Route 66 hummed under my body.
In the back of Dad's old panel truck
I lay on bare, blue and white ticking,
Mattress buttons and little brother
poking my bony ribs.

Tallied white lines
And Guernsey's grazing in pastures
As we headed nowhere, somewhere, anywhere
Dad's rambling soul would take us.

With a dollar in his pocket and a dream in his heart,
The four winds tugged him hither and yon,
Cast us into unknown towns where temporary day jobs, thrift stores
And restrooms with cold water sinks provided vacation basics.

Dad didn't have a dollar to spare
or a dime's worth of sense.
We lodged on the run;
My mattress a communal bed.

Mom wrapped herself in a comma
Around Dad's exclamation point limbs
I snuggled in a fetal question mark,
My brother scrunched in a period at my feet.
Nowadays, when cherry blossoms blanket the ground,
Old Route 66 wraps me up in asphalt arms
Snakes me down winding roads that lead to long ago.
I feel the hum and I must
Go.

Jade Sylvan

Back Home

Driving down an arterial highway,
steel guitar strings picking through the stereo,
windows down in the heat, our hair blows out, not back,
our mouths breathe the molten air.

A tattooed, bearded boy in sandals told me
you miss the scent,
that the smell of Indiana weaves
its way into the fiber of your bones.

In the field with the fireflies, I smell it at dusk in the wet air,
the smell of wooden houses with wooded backyards.

When you are young, you drink beer
from ice kegs in plastic cups in these yards.
You stand around bonfires
with a cigarette somebody rolled for you,
and you try to make the boy you like laugh.

Then you grow and you leave,
pulled by grey matter to grey seas,
by blueprints to big cities.

But trust me, he says,
that sparkling twilight redolence
draws you back.

Draws you back from the inside out,
moves your bones for you
until again you're driving through
the red and orange Jackson Pollack of autumn forests.

My mother, oh my mother had it bad.
Grew up down where they mix whoppers into soft-serve
and the dates end in the beds of pickups.

She showed me the ice cream shop
where she daily bought vanilla malts with her lunch money.
She showed me the farm where she and her best friend,
age eleven, once stole a watermelon, and she showed me
the small Catholic school house
that taught her to carry the guilt
from that summer day through the rest of her life.

She showed me the stone house
her father built with bare hands,
where he lived until her mother threw him out
for coming home drunk one too many times
and knocking her around its walls.

That scent,
firewood asphalt,
bluegrass still-water,
dragonfly sycamore,
it lives in her hard.

Her veins are the fingers of Rivers, White, Wabash, Ohio,
her hair grows the yellow-brown of cornfields,
her eyes injected with the aqua of the summer sky.
She strays but always boomerangs
back to those back roads and malt shops.
When Aunt Jane passes, who will carry
the secret of the blackberry jam?

Home again.
It is a rocky one, but we built it with bare hands.
Its contents change, but the foundation stands.

On the back roads, the stars grow less timorous,
and even the small ones disrobe.

The bed of a pickup is no terrible place
to watch the Milky Way
with your head on a boy's bare shoulder.

No, in one month, he will not love you, but he does tonight.
Past the reservoir in the lime quarries under the stars,
he does.

Anne Brudevold

The Ride

Highway 80, the summer we burned
our high school diplomas, so hot for each other
we thought we could make the old car drive on love.
It was a '54 Ford Thunderbird. We left New York
with one passenger, sex, with us, chatty and insistent.
In Pennsylvania we stopped at a filling station.
"'Cold coke on a hot cock.'
That's a poem, my boyfriend said
resting the can between his legs.
All across Iowa, his hands were on
me and the steering wheel
of the baby blue Ford
that matched the sky we drove toward.
Sex changed like the scenery.
majestic as skyscrapers
arched as bridges
impersonal as corn
quirky as a road runner
dissolute as Las Vegas.
En route, we discovered
we knew each other's bodies,
but we knew nothing about ourselves.
It was awful. So we wrote poems.
He wrote about lifting his scorched face up to the rain
and letting water cool that fire.
I wrote about how his smile divided his face
into sections like grapefruit.
He wrote about my nature, hard like a cactus outside
inside soft and juicy.
In Arizona he proposed
and then dove head-love
into a bed of roses

and smashed his fist against the dashboard
of the blue '54 Thunderbird
and the radio didn't work after that.
Sex became a country
of lengthening shadows.
We wanted to stay tourists
and keep that precious distance it takes to write a poem
and we wanted something we couldn't control
but could put our hands on.
We were afraid, and sex started becoming
something in itself.
In Utah I got out. I was the cold hard stone by the road
I was a place no one could reach
dry in the middle of nowhere
the worthless rock of sex.
And there was the baby blue Ford backing up.
"'Mute white cat,' that's a poem, my boyfriend said.
I got back in the car.
He put his arm around me
and sex became the west.
We were on a record jacket
driving into the brilliant promise of dawn.
In Hollywood the car chipped over broken pavement.
The radio started working again
and we sang along. By night
the moon gave us pale new lives.
By day we had the shattering beauty of the canyons,
the hedges like sandwiches, the plastic coffee cups
with surfaces that glinted like gold.
Above all, in the white trailing pebbles of the world
sex was a great movie scene
and promised more than we did.

Lori Desrosiers

Jalopy

Trailing white smoke down the road
the old Ford hums a rock-n-roll riff,
sways on white wall tires
to the beat of Bumpy and the Pot Holes -
their first album, "Shake it up Baby."
In its fiftieth year, the old jalopy can still
jostle starched skirts over crinoline slips,
bump bow ties above black suspenders.
Another generation of back seat passengers
falls to one side, then the other.

The Gear-Head's Wife's Lament

 Manly men in their man-caves,
garage junkies talking with rumbly voices
to the tune of metal rock 'n roll
about wheels of stainless steels
and semi-hemi trucks with
lifters and shifters and better deals
With dual overhead cams and rams
and flimflams, and traffic jams.
with mufflers and spoilers
and seat-cover lambs,
With spray-painted blocks
and shiny new shocks,
and bad-guy proof locks,
and digital clocks.
They drink bottled beers
discussing the gears
of cars they don't own.
Then, at night, they come home.

Tom Bird

Shop Talk

When I was a young man . . .
All my old friends spoke of muscle
cars as if they were bawdy women
waiting to be had in the back seat.
Voices quivered with anticipation
for that moment of reckless passion.
O Mother Machines! How their mouths gargled
such sweet obscenities! How they throbbed
underneath thin-skinned fingers, tin flesh
vibrating on a bed of leaf springs,
the blast of exhaust– an orgasm of extension!
Alas . . . I sat listening all night to their stories
of conquest with my ignition key in my back pocket;
my lady was a crone gone sour with bashed in teeth,
and slow motion movements. And try as I did,
there was no making myself believe
she wasn't over the hill.

Amy MacLennan

The Beauty Shop

Her name was Opal, and she did
my grandmother's hair,
or "fixed it" as Grandma said,
as if the task of combing
and cutting grey curls
took a bit of engineering,
a knack for making it right.
Every third Saturday
we went downtown,
the sweet sting of shampoo,
straightener, bleach
hitting us well before
we walked into the blast
of moist air and dryers,
Opal waving me to the magazines,
Grandma to the only empty basin.
Opal was all texture,
her face a relief of creases,
her frizzy mane pulled back
to a braided bun. She called
all her customers girls
(I was "young lady")
and they buzzed
about The Edge of Night,
Days of Our Lives, as she rolled
swatches of hair into curlers,
jabbed in bobby pins,
brushed off clippings.
Grandma napped as her hair dried,
and sometimes Opal stepped out
to smoke. Leaning against
the screen door, she flicked ashes

from her Winston, drank coffee with cream
in a styrofoam cup. She rubbed
her wrists with ointment, took an aspirin
every time, and more women came in
for tints, sets, permanent waves,
paid Opal with cash,
placed their hair
in her knotted hands.

Lyn Lifshin

Barbie Looks Up Her Birthday

and feels so
hollow inside,
unfulfilled,
as if all she's
done is change
her clothes.
She wonders a
bout the women's
movement, maybe
she frowns it's
the change and
she hasn't even
had a baby, had
a period, a
hair that was
not in place.
Perfection that
can be shelved,
one yank she
shivers and I'd
be bald, naked.
She flips thru
chapters on
neurosis, wonders
if it's hormones
she lacks. Where
she's been hardly
seems to matter
: the beach, Sun
Valley, Spain.

It's all facade,
going thru the
motions. What
did a wedding
get me she groans,
I never was free
moving as they
said in 1975
but empty, full
of holes, some
thing just for
someone else
to collect.

Sheila Mullen Twyman

On the Fourth Day
New Orleans Flood, September 2005

His hands are grey and puckered,
strange extensions of his brown arms,
he raises them, cup-like near his pursed lips
like he's holding his battered trumpet
and he wails a long, mournful,
ain't nobody coming for me.

He was always amazed his lips could blow his horn
as sweet and easy as spitting out cherry pits,
He marveled the way his long fingers
could flutter endlessly, effortlessly
up and down on the valves
redirecting his breath from the lead pipe
through the brass innards and out the flared bell.

But now his lips are cracked , his hands shaky
from too long sitting in putrid waters,
in the heavy, humid air that takes his breath away.
Not like those nights he used to sit for hours
playing through clouds of weed,
smelling smoldering tobacco and
spilled bourbon drying on tabletops.
Lord, I been sitting in this tree
like a parrot on a perch for days now...
ain't nobody coming for me?

Playing in that jazz band...
what class I had with my hair slicked back,
a suit with black satin stripes down the pants seams
breaking perfectly over spit polish shoes,
jacket lapels with a span of a Madagascar fruit bat.
I played like I talked, loud and free,
next to the guy on drums who played
with a guy who played with the Duke.
That's Ellington, Lord, just in case you forgot.
My music had soul, fine soul...
ain't nobody coming for a fine soul.

Remember that time Satchmo sat in, played
his eight bar intro and we all launched into
East of the Sun, West of the Moon?
Trumpets slid into mellow honey and
the saxs moaned endlessly sorrowful.
I felt like one of the guys manning the oars
the day Jesus came aboard. No offense, Lord,

but in case you're not looking and listening,
seems like ain't nobody coming to get me
but you. Lord...come now
so I can pull real hard on those oars one more time.

Timothy Mason

Baseball Cards

My nephew shows me his baseball card collection.
He brings out binders.
    The mythic sporting images are not perspiring in their
        plastic prophylactics
no card edge is bent or chipped, no gum powder stains show.
They are like bugs on pins or encased in amber
perfectly preserved and perfectly dead.

As he proudly points out the value of his latest page
my mind flashes back to the two battered shoeboxes
              now stashed in my closet,
carrying the dust from many of my lives,
                    My Cards!
Once complete sets '67 and '68
all tattered and scratched, taped, marked in pen
charting the trades and transformations.

                  Me and Danny
we played out a 180 games season with our teams, keeping
    statistics
            we'd take over my TV room, his den,
masking tape bases, our trombone cases making
the walls of The House that Ruth Built
or The Home of The Braves.
With a button ball we'd slide the pitch, roll the dice
        and wear out the knees of many pants sliding
            our cards after them.

        Now, two and a half decades later
I can still see the muscular arms of Aaron,
bat on shoulders, a regular for my guys,
top right side torn from bouncing off the walls,
back side stats worn smooth for speed and swiftness,
    a sure threat to steal a base with the right wrist action.

        My last card in '67 was Mantle,
I'd amassed doubles and triples by the score,
cutting the rookie cards and taping them on
  to expand the roster–
then I got him, a head shot
Mickey Mantle, a face looking stupid–
    I had him before Danny did, kept him for reputation
then dove into the treasure Danny's uncle bestowed.
  Gil Hodges, Ted Williams, Whitey Ford. I got the doubles.
Then going to top that I hit the library,
tearing the pictures from the history books,
wrapping my doubles with Ty Cobb, Josh Gibson, Satchel Paige.
We expanded to the minors, The Mudhens and Bees,
Pioneer League specials Boise, Spokane.
The Negro Leagues. Kansas City Monarchs, Homestead Grays.
We had a card for the commissioner Ford Frick, even umpires
and later, when we were older, cheerleaders
  taken from Playboy.
If we were going to explore the off field dimensions of the game
money was beside the point;
it was a way of life we were after
and when we saw our baseball cards
They were alive.

Charles Salmons

On the 100th Anniversary of the World Series

This year the Boston Red Sox broke the curse.
Beantown's ragtag bunch of beloved boys
put the Bambino's hex in reverse.

Down three games to none, they faced the adverse—
to beat the mighty Yanks, and fought back with poise.
At long last the Red Sox broke the curse.

For Pudge and Yaz, the young fan in the hearse,
for the Splendid Splinter and hopeful schoolboys
they put the Bambino's hex in reverse.

The rough and rugged Sox were a diverse
gang, unlike New York's slick pack of playboys.
But the bedraggled BoSox broke the curse.

In four games no team could ever rehearse,
they whacked Cardinal pitching like breakable toys
and put the Bambino's hex in reverse.

After 86 years they won baseball's purse,
and gave lifelong fans the greatest of joy.
For this year the Red Sox broke the curse
and put the Bambino's hex in reverse.

Caridad McCormick

Things I Didn't Know I Loved

I didn't know I loved America.
Can someone who has cursed America love it?
I who scoff at pledges and anthems,
apple pie folklore carved
on cherry tree trunks
heaped on the backs
of faithful blue oxen,
the lies we tell
to live with ourselves.

Don't think me a rebel.
I remember the words,
and always sing along.

I love America.
Her cities. The way
they wind their way
across a quilted landscape,
dripping with lessons,
like that time
I swallowed 5th Avenue
on foot, tropical blood
chilled by the sun's
way of hiding behind buildings,
biding its time
immune to the wild eyed
Medusa there, propped up
against an alabaster edge
skin taut against her bones,
soup bowl hollows
collecting rain
beneath the collar
of her Glad bag chic–

plastic fashioned into a dress,
fringed packing tape
cinched at the waist,
tears like diamonds
freezing on her face.

More than those
who stepped over her
who ignored her
who tightened
their leather, their minks,
their impeccable suedes,
I remember the woman
who stooped beside her.

Who said
Can I help you?
Who asked
What's wrong,
Sister, what's wrong?

Who did
not falter in the stink
and wail of humiliation.

Who called
for help as I made
my way away,
spinning through
the crowd
vision blurred,
too cold to stop
or turn around,
all pity,
no purpose,
walking,
walking.

Kit Wallach

Johnny Appleseed

I.
More important than the footprints
He left in the new dark earth
Was the way the soles of his feet looked
As he lifted them:
The walking,
The leaving,
The little he had,
That he was always alone.

We loved him for the figure he cut
Against the low horizon–
Sky burning range behind him, his
Tin cup silhouette.

II.
Johnny is not names Appletree.
Apple seed, wooden teardrop lying still
In the snow cave of apple flesh,
Like a hibernating child.

The teeth of the world rip at the skin
Thin as the breathing in your back,
Thin as the air that comes through the window casings.
The lips and teeth of the world crush
The meat of the apple into drift ice.

Apple seed, you and your brothers lie still as the
Five points of a star, rocking gently
In your apple cradles,
Deep and quiet inside the eating apple–
If the teeth of the world ever reach you
The tongue will spit you back out–

III.
A young woman, a farmer's wife,
Kneads the knuckles of her hands in the folds of her apron,
And looks out the window to see
Johnny, patron saint of introduced species,
Of strangers, of men who dream of raising
Red mountains from the broad swell of the plains.

He is just leaving. The pan on his head
Makes him look like a poorly equipped soldier.
As he walks, his hands drip seeds.
They form a dotted line on the map of his travels.

A hundred years pass.
The trees have become, in spring, old
Japanese men, stretching their arms with fresh new leaves,
After the long winter of wanting
To draw up into themselves all of their limbs.

In late summer, green fruit hangs heavy as earlobes,
And in the fall, an apple with a bloom of red
On its spotted skin transfers from a low branch
To the palm of a child, who later that day
Will feed it to a mare with soft lips
And wet nostrils, and when she nuzzle his hand
He will feel, wondering, his first true moment of human
Inadequacy–and the horse and the tree are the same
Stooping creature; gentle with the child,
Looking him in the eye like a lover.

In the old apple trees lining the road
We see nothing left of Johnny, save maybe
That look of exposure to the elements, and perhaps
One long, soft kiss he might have shared
With the farmer's wife, before he remembered
He wasn't any good at talking to people, and moved
Quietly along down the land, his pockets always full.

Contributors

Jean Meyer Aloe is enrolled in the M.A. program in Creative Writing at Manhattanville College, Purchase, NY and has been published in *The Christian Science Monitor, Poetry of the Tsunami, The Best of the Fairfield Review, Bottle Rockets, Writers' Journal,* and *The Red Clay Review.*

Madeline Artenberg's poetry has appeared in many publications, such as *Margie*. Her book, *Awakened*, was published by Rogue Scholars

Tom Bird has been writing poetry on and off for thirty plus years (beginning in the Army) and was recently published in *Relief Journal*. He is the pastor of a small church in the Adirondaks of New York State.

Tony Brown, of Worcester MA, has been writing and performing poetry for over thirty years. He was recently named *Poet Laureate of the Blogosphere* for 2008, for whatever that's worth.

Anne Brudevold owns EdenWatersPress. She has published poems and stories widely, and is publishing a novel online with Wilderness House Press. She lives in Boston, but her soul is in the Pioneer Valley.

Tom Chandler is Poet Laureate of Rhode Island emeritus.

Lucille Lang Day has published seven poetry collections and chapbooks, most recently *The Book of Answers* (2006) and *God of the Jellyfish* (2007).

Lori Desrosiers is a native of New York City, but now calls Westfield, MA her home. She has published her poems in *Big City Lit, Blue Fifth Review, Ballard Street Poetry Journal, The Equinox, Silkworm* and others. She is a 2008 MFA candidate in Poetry at New England College in New Hampshire.

Peter Dolack is a poet, essayist, photographer and activist in Brooklyn, N.Y., who sometimes finds himself on the road, but not often enough.

Gretchen Fletcher grew up when patriotism was part of the zeitgeist. Her father made sure she traveled the USA. She recently won the Poetry Society of America's Bright Lights Big Verse competition and read her winning poem in the midst of Times Square, the heart of America, while being projected on the Jumbotron.

John Flynn has published three chapbooks of poetry: *Westbound Freight* and *A Dozen Lemons In Autotropolis* were with Pudding House. His poetry has earned awards from Peace Corps Writers and Readers, Worcester County Poetry Association, and New England Poetry Club.

Suzanne Frank's work has appeared in *ACM, Power Lines* (Tia Chucha Press), *Stray Bullets, A Celebration of Chicago Saloon Poetry* (Tia Chucha Press). She lives in Chicago where she works in landscape design and horteculture.

Lewis Gardner's poems and plays have been published and performed throughout the U.S. and Europe. The story of Aunt Priudence happened exactly as stated.

Sarah Getty's second book of poems, *Bring Me Her Heart*, was published last year and received Pulitzer and NBA nominations.

Ted Giovannini is a working class poet, single parent, loving grandparent, leftist, and atheist living in the slums of Brockton, Massachusetts. He needs to speak out, learn and be part of the tidal wave of artistic hope for the future.

Sharon Lynn Griffiths is a resident (body and soul) of Jersey City. Her poems have appeared in *Long Shot, The Paterson Literary Review, Exit 13, the Cafe Review, the California Quarterly, Lips, Blue Collar Review*, and *The Comstock Review*. She works as an adult literacy teacher in NYC.

F.I. Goldhaber has been a professional writer for more than a quarter century. Her stories, poems, and articles have been published in magazines, newspapers, and anthologies. Her collection *Pairs of Poems*, is available from Uncial Press.

Julia Gordon-Bramer's award-winning poetry and prose has appeared in *Rainy Day, Carve, Santa Fe Writers Project Literary Journal*, and others.

Melissa Guillet founded Sacred Fools Press as a way of promoting old and new voices and exploring poetry thematically. She has been published in numerous anthologies and journals, including *The Cherry Blossom Review, Lalitamba, Nth Position, Scrivener's Pen,* and *Women. Period.* She teaches art and lives with poet Ryk McIntyre and their toddler.

Paul Hamill has published in many journals including *Georgia Review, Southern Review*, and *Poetry*. He is current Poet Laureate of Tompkins County in upstate New York, where he works at Ithaca College

Bob Hoeppner lives in Southwick, MA. He's been published in various places, in print and online.

Thomas D. Jones is author of *Genealogy X*, his first book of poetry published by The Poets Press, Providence, RI.

Elizabeth Kerlikowske teaches in Battle Creek, Michigan, where it always smells like morning, a town she met in commericials during *The Beverly Hillbillies*.

Jim Lanier lives in the foothills of California, off the grid, in a straw bale house he built with his wife, Becky. He's been published in *Rattlesnake Review* and in Indiana University South Bend's *Analecta*.

David Lawton is a spoken word artist performing in New York City venues, utilizing his background in theatre and music. His website is www.myspace.com/lawtonium.

Valerie Lawson's poetry has been published in literary journals, anthologies, and web sites. Her chapbook, *Ribbon Anvil*, was a finalist for Best Poetry Publication at the 2002 Cambridge Poetry Awards. Lawson was the individual winner of Female Spoken Word and Best Narrative Poem at the Cambridge Poetry Awards in 2004. She released a new book of poems, *Dog Watch*, in 2007.

Lyn Lifshin has published more than 120 books of poetry, including *Marilyn Monroe* and *Blue Tattoo*. She won awards for her non-fiction and edited four anthologies of women's writing including *Tangled Vines, Ariadne's Thread* and *Lips Unsealed*.

Stephen Lindow earned his MFA in 2004 from the University of MA–Amherst, interned at the MA Review, and toured with Poetry Alive, Inc. He teaches 8th grade English in Springfield, MA and owns a spaceship.

Joanne Lowery's poems have appeared in many literary magazines, including *Birmingham Poetry Review, Smartish Pace, Passages North, Atlanta Review*, and *Poetry East*. She lives in Michigan.

Amy MacLennan's work has been published in *Cimarron Review, Folio, Wisconsin Review, Rattle* and *South Dakota Review*.

Timothy Mason has been actively promoting poetry and folk music in greater Boston since the mid 1980's. A member of the first National Poetry Slam Team from Boston in 1991 and the first Worcester Team in 1993, he honed his performance style around the campfires of the fabled Kerrville Folk Festival, giving the songwriters a run for their money.

Marty McConnell received her MFA from Sarah Lawrence College and is a director of the louderARTS Project, a New York City-based literary nonprofit. Her work has been published in numerous journals and anthologies. She sleeps in Brooklyn.

Caridad McCormick's poetry has appeared or is forthcoming in numerous journals and anthologies including *Crab Orchard Review, MiPoesias, The Seattle Review, Slipstream, CALYX, Spillway, The Pedestal, The Sun, Fifth Wednesday Journal, Just Like A Girl: A Manifesta, Susan B. and Me: An International Collection of Writing*, and *Her Mark, 2009*. She received the Florida Individual Artist Fellowship in poetry in 2007 and was a finalist for the Rita Dove Poetry Award in 2008 and 2006. McCormick is a professor of English at Miami Dade College and a staff columnist for *Oranges and Sardines, A Quarterly Art and Poetry Journal*. Her chapbook *Visionware* is forthcoming from Finishing Line Press.

Ryk McIntyre is a poet, columnist and workshop leader, living in Providence, RI. He tours all over the country and then comes back to a loving home.

Artie Moffa gets paid to write limericks for video games.

Victoria Muñoz is a singer/songwriter, poet and music therapist. She has featured throughout the East Coast, including the York Arts Festival. She is also a member of the "Not Just *Any* Tom, Vic and Terri Poetry Ensemble." Publications include her chapbook, *During Your Reading*, bentpinquarterly.net, and *New Songs from the Meadows, an Anthology from the Wood Memorial Library*.

Linda O'Connell's work has appeared in periodicals, anthologies, literary magazines, numerous *Chicken Soup for the Soul* collections, *Voices of Breast Cancer, Voices of Autism, Elder Wisdom, Silver Boomers, Mom Writers, Boomer Women Speak, The Mochila Review, Flashquake, Andwerve, Reminisce, Reader's Digest, True Love, Sasee, New Verse News* and more.

Jeff Poniewaz. Allen Ginsberg has praised Jeff Poniewaz's poetry for its "impassioned prescient Whitmanesque/Thoreauvian verve and wit."

Kim Roberts is the author of two books of poetry, *The Kimnama* (Vrzhu Press, 2007), and *The Wishbone Galaxy* (WWPH, 1994) and has been published in *Southwest Review, Ohio Review, Malahat Review, No Tell Motel,* and *New Letters*. She edits an online journal, *Beltway Poetry Quarterly*, and co-edits the *Delaware Poetry Review*.

Helen Ruggieri has published work in *Pomeleon, Umbrella, Cezanne's Carrot, Hawaii Pacific Review, Cream City Review, del sol review, Valparaiso, Poetry Midwest*, and elsewhere. She lives in Olean, NY and watches too much TV.

Michele "Mitz" Sackman, from Murphys, California, burned all her poetry at age 15 to prevent the reoccurrence of her younger sisters' dramatic reading of the same for the neighborhood children. At age 45, with the sisters currently employed as lawyers and held to standards by the Bar Association, she picked up her pen again and hasn't stopped since.

Charles Salmons is an assistant editor with McGraw-Hill Education and an adjunct at Columbus State Community College in Columbus, Ohio. His poems have appeared in *The Offbeat, Paradigm,* and *The Best of Ohio Poetry Day 2006.*

Hal Sirowitz is the former Poet Laureate of Queens, New York.

David Lee Summers is the author of four novels and numerous short stories and poems. He lives in New Mexico.

Jade Sylvan has been published in *The Ibbetson Journal* and *Word Riot.*

Sheila Mullen Twyman's poetry and short fiction have been published in literary journals and anthologies. She has two poetry collections. She hosts "Poetry Under the Trees," an annual open mic gathering during the Marshfield Arts Festival, and produces and hosts "Egads, It's Poetry," for the MA Radio Network for the Blind, which features local poets reading their work.

Wendy Vardaman has a Ph.D. in English from University of Pennsylvania. Her poems, reviews and interviews have appeared in *Poet Lore, Main Street Rag, Nerve Cowboy, Free Verse, Pivot, Wisconsin People & Ideas, Women's Review of Books* and *Portland Review Literary Journal*. She has received several Pushcart Prize nominations and was runner up in 2004 for the Council for Wisconsin Writers' Lorine Niedecker Award.

Jennifer Wallace teaches in Baltimore. An editor at *The Cortland Review* and at *Toadlily Press*, her poems have appeared in literary journals and on radio.

Kit Wallach is a member of the all-woman Hungry Raptor Squad who represented a coalition of Amherst colleges at *Brave New Voices*, the college national poetry slam.

Laura Lee Washburn's most recent collection is *This Good Warm Place, Expanded 10th Ann. Ed.* (March Street Press). Her first book, *Watching the Contortionists*, won the 1996 Palanquin Press Chapbook Award. Her poems have been anthologized in *Starting Rumors: America's Next Generation of Writers* (Pinyon Press 1999). She is an editorial board member of the Woodley Memorial Press and is the Director of Creative Writing at Pittsburg State University. She resides in Kansas with writer Roland Sodowsky.

Bruce Weber is the author of four books of poetry, most recently *Poetic Justice* (Ikon Press: New York, 2004)

Lenore Weiss was a finalist in the 2008 Pablo Neruda Prize for Poetry. Her latest chapbook is *Sh'ma Yis'rael* (Pudding House Publications). Lenore serves as the fiction editor of the *November 3rd Club*, an online publication that explores "Literary Values in a Political Age."

David Wolf is the author of three poetry collections (*Open Season, The Moment Forever* and *Sablier*) and teaches at Simpson College.

Acknowledgments:

All previously published work reprinted by permission of the authors.

"Chosen Seats" first appeared in *Awakened*, poems by Madeline Artenberg and Iris N. Schwartz (Rogue Scholars Press, 2006).

Tony Brown's "Where Do You Live?" was originally published in the chapbook *Americanized* (Loyal Weasel Press, 2007); it also appears on the CD of the same name from *Duende*, Brown's collaboration with Steven Cafaro on bass and guitar.

Tom Chandler's poem "Jerimoth Hill" previously appeared in *Across State Lines*, the 2003 anthology of the American Poetry & Literacy Project.

Lucille Lang Day's "710 Ashbury, 1967" was first published in *Re)verb*, Issue 2 (Summer 2003).

John Flynn's "In Praise of Boston Aunts" first appeared in *Ibbetson Street Press*, a journal out of Somerville, MA.

"Aunt Prudence" by Lewis Gardner has never been published, although it is part of a stage work called *Tales of the Middlesex Canal*, which has been widely performed. "Pennies" was published in *The New York Times*.

F.I. Goldhaber's "The Mall" will appear in her collection *Pairs of Poems* (Uncial Press, 2008).

Amy MacLennan's "The Beauty Shop" was first published in *Blue Arc West, An Anthology of California Poets* (Tebot Bach, 2006).

Tim Mason's "Baseball Cards" first appeared in his chapbook *Gently, Like Water, Cracking Stone*; an audio version is available on his CD *Bloodlines*.

"Fresco From Summer" first appeared in Victoria Muñoz's chapbook, *During Your Reading*.

Kim Roberts' "Lydia E. Pinkham's Vegetable Compound" first appeared in *Attic, Maryland State Poetry and Literary Society* (Issue 2, September 2007). Her poem "New Haven" originally was published in *The Broadkill Review* (Vol. 1, No. 1, January 2007).

David Lee Summers' poem "Racing Amtrak" first appeared in the *The Ink Spot* (2005), a small chapbook of poems produced annually by *The Ink*, a local arts newspaper published in Las Cruces, New Mexico.

"A Slow-Filling Cloud", by Jennifer Wallace, was published in the journal *Passager* (Spring, 2008).

Bruce Weber's "Toy Soldiers" first appeared in the anthology *Will Work for Peace* (Zeropanik Press, 1999).

David Wolf's poem "Maneuvers" first appeared in *Poet & Critic* Vol. 24, No.2 (Winter 1993). The poem also appears in his collection *Open Season*.

www.ingramcontent.com/pod-product-compliance
Lightning Source LLC
Chambersburg PA
CBHW032139040426
42449CB00005B/313